A Quotes Happiness

Gregory F. Roberts

Copyright © 2020 Gregory F. Roberts

All rights reserved.

ISBN: 9798569571499

DEDICATION

For Nicholas, Hayden, and Olivia. Thank you for bringing joy and happiness to my life. I hope that you can find happiness in your lives too.

A Dozen Dozen Quotes: Happiness

CONTENTS

	Acknowledgments	i
1	Happiness Is…	1
2	Quotes	2
3	The Boring Stuff	146
4	Author Index	147

ACKNOWLEDGMENTS

I would like to acknowledge Michele Land for the cover photograph. Trading nature and flower pictures with you gives me a smile I hope it give you a smile too. Thank you.

1 HAPPINESS IS...

What is happiness? Is happiness something you have or don't have? Is happiness a destination to strive towards? Can happiness last or is it fleeting? The dozen dozen quotes about happiness that fill the rest of these pages might help you answer these questions. Often times, I think we are happy, but just don't slow down enough to recognize that we are. So, stop and take a moment to assess your current state of mind. Are you happy? If so, GREAT! Keep that positive energy flowing. If not, what would make you happy? Thinking about what would make you happy can just...well...make you happy. The Law of Attraction will give you what you ask for. Ask. Believe. Receive. And, if you need some inspiration about happiness, well, I have a 144 quotes for you, so keep reading.

If you don't design your own life plan, chances are you'll fall into someone else's plan. And guess what they have planned for you? Not much.

— **Jim Rohn**

Enjoy it. Because it's happening.

— **Stephen Chbosky**

Happiness is not something ready made. It comes from your own actions.

— **Dalai Lama**

Don't wait around for other people to be happy for you. Any happiness you get you've got to make yourself.

— **Alice Walker**

What we think determines what happens to us, so if we want to change our lives, we need to stretch our minds.

— **Wayne Dyer**

If you want to be happy, set a goal that commands your thoughts, liberates your energy, and inspires your hopes.

— **Andrew Carnegie**

Be happy with what you have an are, be generous with both and you won't have to hunt for happiness.

— **William E. Gladstone**

Don't postpone joy until you have learned all of your lessons. Joy is your lesson.

— **Alan Cohen**

Happiness is a gift and the trick is not to expect it, but to delight in it when it comes.

— **Charles Dickens**

Joy is more divine than sorrow; for joy is bread, and sorrow is medicine.

— Henry Ward Beecher

Life is 10% what happens to you and 90% how you respond to it.

— **Lou Holtz**

Love is trembling happiness.

— **Khalil Gibran**

Happiness? That's nothing more than health and a poor memory.

— **Albert Schweitzer**

Life is short. Smile while you still have teeth.

— **Unknown**

Today is life – the only life you are sure of. Make the most of today. Get interested in something. Shake yourself awake. Develop a hobby. Let the winds of enthusiasm sweep through you. Live today with gusto.

— **Dale Carnegie**

Security is when everything is settled, when nothing can happen to you; security is the denial of life.

— **Germaine Greer**

To forget oneself is to be happy.

— **Robert Louis Stevenson**

Happiness does not lie in happiness, but in the achievement of it.

— **Fyodor Dostoevsky**

There can be no happiness if the things we believe in are different from the things we do.

— **Freya Stark**

It is not God's will merely that we should be happy, but that we should make ourselves happy.

— **Immanuel Kant**

Enjoyment is just the sound of being centered.

— **Bhagwan Shree Rajneesh**

Finding happiness is easy: stop being busy.

— **Maxime Lagacé**

Say no more often so you can say yes to what's important.

— **Maxime Lagacé**

Three grand essentials to happiness in this life are something to do, something to love, and something to hope for.

— **Joseph Addison**

Don't cry because it's over, smile because it happened.

— **Ludwig Jacobowski**

To be able to throw one's self away for the sake of a moment, to be able to sacrifice years for a woman's smile - that is happiness.

— **Hermann Hesse**

If you want to be happy, be.

— Leo Tolstoy

I must learn to be content with being happier than I deserve.

— **Jane Austin**

Happiness is not being pained in body or troubled in mind.

— **Thomas Jefferson**

The happiness of a man in this life does not consist in the absence but in the mastery of his passions.

— **Alfred Lord Tennyson**

Happiness is inward, and not outward; and so, it does not depend on what we have, but on what we are.

— **Henry Van Dyke**

He who lives in harmony with himself lives in harmony with the universe.

— **Marcus Aurelius**

It is difficult to find happiness within oneself, but it is impossible to find it anywhere else.

— **Arthur Schopenhauer**

Happiness is the default state. It's what's there when you remove the sense that something is missing in life.

— **Naval Ravikant**

Our happiness depends on wisdom all the way.

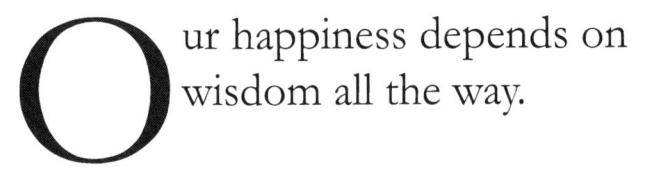

— **Sophocles**

Life in common among people who love each other is the ideal of happiness.

— **George Sand**

It is the very mark of the spirit of rebellion to crave for happiness in this life.

— **Henrik Ibsen**

Happiness cannot be traveled to, owned, earned, worn or consumed. Happiness is the spiritual experience of living every minute with love, grace, and gratitude.

— **Denis Waitley**

Happiness is a continuation of happenings which are not resisted.

— **Deepak Chopra**

Happiness is a by-product. You cannot pursue it by itself.

— **Sam Levenson**

If we would just slow down, happiness would catch up to us.

— **Richard Carlson**

Anything you are good at contributes to happiness.

— **Bertrand Russell**

A truly happy person is one who can enjoy the scenery while on a detour.

— **Unknown**

Happiness is found in doing, not merely possessing.

— **Napoleon Hill**

There is only one happiness in this life, to love and be loved.

— **George Sand**

To be happy, you must fancy that everything you have is a gift, and you the chosen, though you worked your tail off for every bit of it.

— **Robert Brault**

It is the chiefest point of happiness that a man is willing to be what he is.

— **Desiderius Erasmus**

Success is getting what you want. Happiness is wanting what you get.

— **Dale Carnegie**

The advantages of a bad memory is that one enjoys several times the good things for the first time.

— **Friedrich Nietzsche**

Happiness is like those palaces in fairy tales whose gates are guarded by dragons: we must fight in order to conquer it.

— **Alexandre Dumas**

Nothing prevents happiness like the memory of happiness.

— **Andre Gide**

True happiness arises, in the first place, from the enjoyment of one's self.

— Joseph Addison

Boredom is feeling that everything is a waste of time…serenity, that nothing is.

— **Thomas Szasz**

We don't laugh because we are happy — we're happy because we laugh.

— **William James**

You can only have bliss if you don't chase it.

— **Henepola Gunaratana**

When someone told me I lived in a fantasy land, I nearly fell off my unicorn.

— Unknown

Happiness doesn't depend on any external conditions, it is governed by our mental attitude.

— **Dale Carnegie**

You can be happy where you are.

— **Joel Osteen**

The constant of happiness is curiosity.

— **Alice Munro**

Happiness is the state of consciousness which proceeds from the achievement of one's values.

— **Ayn Rand**

The most worth-while thing is to try to put happiness into the lives of others.

— **Robert Baden-Powell**

Happiness is when what you think, what you say, and what you do are in harmony.

— **Mahatma Gandhi**

What we call the secret to happiness is no more a secret than our willingness to choose life.

— Leo Buscaglia

Lovers who love truly do not write down their happiness.

— **Anatole France**

The greatest secret to happiness and peace is letting every life situation be what it is, instead of what you think it should be. Then, make the very best of it.

— **Thibaut**

Expecting life to treat you well because you are a good person is like expecting an angry bull not to charge because you are a vegetarian.

— **Shari R. Barr**

Sometimes we don't find the thing that will make us happy because we can't give up the thing that was supposed to.

— **Robert Brault**

In the end, it's not the years in your life that count. It's the life in your years.

— **Abraham Lincoln**

It is only to the happy that tears are a luxury.

— **Thomas Moore**

The only way to find true happiness is to risk being completely cut open.

— **Chuck Palahniuk**

For every minute you are angry you lose sixty seconds of happiness.

— Ralph Waldo Emerson

Happiness seems made to be shared.

— **Pierre Corneille**

Seek it outside and you'll be exhausted. Seek it inside you'll find a path.

— **Maxime Lagacé**

The secret to happiness is to admire without desiring

— Carl Sandburg

Plenty of people miss their share of happiness, not because they never found it, but because they didn't stop to enjoy it.

— **William Feather**

The deepest satisfaction you'll find will be when you give all you've got on one thing, or when you'll do absolutely nothing and accept life as it is. Think On and Off. Avoid the middle.

— **Maxime Lagacé**

The best way to pay for a lovely moment is to enjoy it.

— **Richard Bach**

Happiness in this world, when it comes, comes incidentally. Make it the object of pursuit, and it leads us a wild-goose chase, and is never attained.

— **Nathaniel Hawthorne**

Folks are usually about as happy as they make their minds up to be.

— **Abraham Lincoln**

Thousands of candles can be lit from a single candle, and the life of the candle will not be shortened. Happiness never decreases by being shared.

— **Buddha**

We can't direct the wind, but we can adjust the sails.

— **Unknown**

We are no longer happy so soon as we wish to be happier.

— **Walter Savage Landor**

Ask yourself whether you are happy and you cease to be so.

— **John Stuart Mill**

Happiness is a direction, not a place.

— **Sydney J. Harris**

Happiness: A butterfly, which when pursued, seems always just beyond your grasp; but if you sit down quietly, may alight upon you.

— **Nathanial Hawthorne**

Happiness makes up in height for what it lacks in length.

— **Robert Frost**

Cry. Forgive. Learn. Move on. Let your tears water the seeds of your future happiness.

— **Steve Maraboli**

Happy is the man who has broken the chains which hurt the mind, and has given up worrying once and for all.

— **Ovid**

I, not events, have the power to make me happy or unhappy today. I can choose which it shall be. Yesterday is dead, tomorrow hasn't arrived yet. I have just one day, today, and I'm going to be happy in it.

— **Groucho Marx**

There is only one way to happiness and that is to cease worrying about things which are beyond the power of our will.

— **Epictetus**

So we shall let the reader answer this question for himself: who is the happier man, he who has braved the storm of life and lived or he who has stayed securely on shore and merely existed?

— **Hunter S. Thompson**

Happiness depends on ourselves.

— **Aristotle**

People don't notice if it is winter or summer when they're happy.

— **Anton Chekhov**

Blessed are those who can give without remembering and take without forgetting.

— **Bernard Meltzer**

One of the keys to happiness is a bad memory.

— **Rita Mae Brown**

Happiness, not in a another place but this place...not for another hour, but this hour.

— **Walt Whitman**

Every gift from a friend is a wish for your happiness.

— **Richard Bach**

Happiness is having a scratch for every itch.

— **Ogden Nash**

Happiness is not a goal; it is a by-product.

— **Eleanor Roosevelt**

In every part and corner of our life, to lose oneself is to be a gainer; to forget oneself is to be happy.

— **Robert Louis Stevenson**

On the whole, the happiest people seem to be those who have no particular cause for being happy except that they are so.

— **William R. Inge**

Happiness? A good cigar, a good meal, a good cigar and a good woman - or a bad woman; it depends on how much happiness you can handle.

— **George Burns**

Happiness does not lead to gratitude. Gratitude leads to happiness.

— **David Steindl-Rast**

Now and then it's good to pause in our pursuit of happiness and just be happy.

— **Guillaume Apollinaire**

Time you enjoy wasting is not wasted time.

— **Marthe Troly-Curtin**

All who joy would win must share it. Happiness was born a twin.

— **Lord Byron**

Be happy. It really annoys negative people.

— **Ricky Gervais**

In times of joy, all of us wished we possessed a tail we could wag.

— **W. H. Auden**

That's your unlimited desires that are clouding your peace, your happiness.

— **Naval Ravikant**

Your success and happiness are forgiven you only if you generously consent to share them.

— **Albert Camus**

Everyone chases after happiness, not noticing that happiness is right at their heels.

— **Bertolt Brecht**

The art of being happy lies in the power of extracting happiness from common things.

— **Henry Ward Beecher**

Happiness is a function of accepting what is.

— **Werner Erhard**

It is in the compelling zest of high adventure and of victory, and it creative action, that man finds his supreme joys.

— Antoine de Saint-Exupery

Happiness is not doing fun things. Happiness is doing meaningful things.

— **Maxime Lagacé**

All happiness or unhappiness solely depends upon the quality of the object to which we are attached by love.

— **Baruch Spinoza**

The ultimate value of life depends upon awareness and the power of contemplation rather than upon mere survival.

— **Aristotle**

To describe happiness is to diminish it.

— **Stendhal**

Not wanting something is as good as having it.

— **Naval Ravikant**

If you want others to be happy, practice compassion. If you want to be happy, practice compassion.

— **Dalai Lama**

There are people who can do all fine and heroic things but one - keep from telling their happiness to the unhappy.

— Mark Twain

Nobody can be uncheered with a balloon.

— A.A. Milne (Pooh)

Happy is he who learns to bear what he cannot change.

— **Friedrich Schiller**

Research has shown that the best way to be happy is to make each day happy.

— **Deepak Choprak**

Happiness isn't something you experience; it's something you remember.

— **Oscar Levant**

There are two ways to be happy: improve your reality, or lower your expectations.

— **Jodi Picoult**

It's the moments that I stopped just to be, rather than do, that have given me true happiness.

— **Richard Branson**

The happiness of your life depends upon the quality of your thoughts: therefore, guard accordingly, and take care that you entertain no notions unsuitable to virtue and reasonable nature.

— **Marcus Aurelius**

Happiness is the only good. The time to be happy is now. The place to be happy is here. The way to be happy is to make others so.

— **Robert Green Ingersoll**

Action may not always bring happiness; but there is no happiness without action.

— **Benjamin Disraeli**

Don't let your happiness depend on something you may lose.

— C.S. Lewis

We forge the chains we wear in life.

— **Charles Dickens**

The best way to cheer yourself it to try to cheer someone else up.

— **Mark Twain**

To be without some of the things you want is an indispensable part of happiness.

— **Bertrand Russell**

Happiness does not consist in pastimes and amusements but in virtuous activities.

— **Aristotle**

If you aren't grateful for what you already have, what makes you think you would be happy with more?

— **Roy T. Bennett**

Most of us believe in trying to make other people happy only if they can be happy in ways which we approve.

— **Robert S. Lynd**

God, grant me the serenity to accept the things I cannot change, the courage to change the things I can, and the wisdom to know the difference.

— **Reinhold Niebuhr**

Life is really simple, but we insist on making it complicated.

— **Confucius**

Be happy for this moment.
This moment is your life.

— **Omar Khayyam**

A sure way to lose happiness, I found, is to want it at the expense of everything else.

— **Bette Davis**

Happiness is not a matter of intensity but of balance, order, rhythm and harmony.

— **Thomas Merton**

If you find happiness, people may be jealous. Be happy anyway.

— **Mother Teresa**

Is it not clear, however, that bliss and envy are the numerator and denominator of the fraction called happiness?

— **Yevgeny Zamyatin**

3 THE BORING STUFF

So what did you think of the quotes? Did you start from the beginning and read straight through to the end? Did you open a page randomly and start from there? Did you think about what the authors were really trying to say? For instance, did you consider what Napoleon Hill (page 45) said with regards to happiness being something you have or don't have? Did you consider what Denis Waitly (page 49) said about happiness being a destination to strive towards? I intended this book to be inspirational for you, not a lesson book. There are no right or wrong answers to the question of "Happiness", only those that you learn for yourself. I will leave you with what I started you out with: Ask. Believe. Receive. If we all practiced the Law of Attraction, we could change the world for the better.

4 AUTHOR INDEX

Addison, Joseph	25, 53
Apollinaire, Guillaume	105
Aristotle	93, 118, 136
Auden, W.H.	109
Aurelius, Marcus	33, 129
Austin, Jane	29
Bach, Richard	78, 98
Baden-Powell, Robert	62
Barr, Shari R.	67
Beecher, Henry Ward	11, 113
Bennett, Roy T.	137
Branson, Richard	128
Brault, Robert	47, 68
Brecht, Bertolt	112
Brown, Rita Mae	96
Buddha	81
Burns, George	103
Buscaglia, Leo	64
Camus, Albert	111
Carlson, Richard	42
Carnegie, Andrew	7
Carnegie, Dale	16, 49, 58
Chbosky, Stephen	3
Chekhov, Anton	94
Choprak, Deepak	40, 125
Cohen, Alan	9
Confucius	140

Corneille, Pierre	73
Dalai Lama	4, 121
Davis, Bette	142
Dickens, Charles	10, 133
Disraeli, Benjamin	131
Dostoevsky, Fyodor	19
Dumas, Alexandre	51
Dyer, Wayne	6
Emerson, Ralph Waldo	72
Epictetus	91
Erasmus, Desiderius	48
Erhard, Werner	114
Feather, William	76
France, Anatole	65
Frost, Robert	87
Gandhi, Mahatma	63
Gervais, Ricky	108
Gibran, Khalil	13
Gide, Andre	52
Gladstone, William E.	8
Greer, Germaine	17
Gunaratana, Henepola	56
Harris, Sydney J.	85
Hawthorne, Nathaniel	79, 86
Hesse, Hermann	27
Hill, Napoleon	45
Holtz, Lou	12
Ibsen, Henrik	38
Inge, William R.	102
Ingersoll, Robert Green	130
Jacobowski, Ludwig	26
James, William	55
Jefferson, Thomas	30
Kant, Immanuel	21
Khayyam, Omar	141
Lagacé, Maxime	23, 24, 74, 77, 116
Landor, Walter Savage	83
Levant, Oscar	126

Levenson, Sam	41
Lewis, C.S.	132
Lincoln, Abraham	69, 80
Lord Byron	107
Lynd, Robert S.	138
Maraboli, Steve	88
Marx, Groucho	90
Meltzer, Bernard	95
Merton, Thomas	143
Mill, John Stuart	84
Milne, A.A. (Pooh)	123
Moore, Thomas	70
Munro, Alice	60
Nash, Ogden	99
Niebuhr, Reinhold	139
Nietzsche, Friedrich	50
Osteen, Joel	59
Ovid	89
Palahniuk, Chuck	71
Picoult, Jodi	127
Rajneesh, Bhagwan Shree	22
Rand, Ayn	61
Ravikant, Naval	35, 110, 120
Rohn, Jim	2
Roosevelt, Eleanor	100
Russell, Bertrand	43, 135
Sand, George	37, 46
Sandburg, Carl	75
Schiller, Friedrich	124
Schopenhauer, Arthur	34
Schweitzer, Albert	14
Sophocles	36
Spinoza, Baruch	117
Stark, Freya	20
Steindl-Rast, David	104
Stendhal	119
Stevenson, Robert Louis	18, 101
Szasz, Thomas	54

Tennyson, Alfred Lord	31
Teresa, Mother	144
Thibaut	66
Thompson, Hunter S.	92
Tolstoy, Leo	28
Troly-Curtin, Marthe	106
Twain, Mark	122, 134
Unknown	15, 44, 57, 82
Van Dyke, Henry	32
Waitley, Denis	39
Walker, Alice	5
Whitman, Walt	97
Zamyatin, Yevgeny	145
de Saint-Exupery, Antoine	115

ABOUT THE AUTHOR

Gregory F. Roberts is a linguistic expert, with a specialization in onomastics and sociolinguistics. He has traveled the world providing his subject mater expertise for a wide variety of commercial and government clients. He is a serial entrepreneur and founder and CEO of IMT Holdings, Corp. and Rosoka Software, Inc. Rosoka is a premier natural language processing software company located in Herndon, VA.